Mastering Math is designed to help children build early mathematical skills. Many exercises reinforce number and shape recognition. Other activities provide practice in such basic skills as addition, subtraction, and story problems. Children also are introduced to fractions, telling time and counting money.

Table of Contents

Glossary

Addition. "Putting together" or adding two or more numbers to find the sum. For example, 3 + 5 = 8.

Circle. A figure that is round. It looks like this: ○.

Diamond. A figure with four sides of the same length. Its corners form points at the top, sides, and bottom. It looks like this: ◇.

Digit. The symbols used to write numbers: 0, 1, 2, 3, 4, 5, 6, 7, 8, and 9.

Dime. Ten cents. It is written **10¢** or **$.10**.

Fraction. A number that names part of a whole, such as **1/2** or **1/3**.

Half-hour. Thirty minutes. When the long hand of the clock is pointing to the six, the time is on the half-hour. It is written **:30**, such as **5:30**.

Hour. Sixty minutes. The short hand of a clock tells the hour.

Nickel. Five cents. It is written **5¢** or **$.05**.

Ordinal number. Numbers that indicate order in a series, such as first, second, or third.

Oval. A figure that is egg-shaped. It looks like this: ⬭

Penny. One cent. It is written **1¢** or **$.01**.

Place Value. The value of a digit, or numeral, shown by where it is in the number. For example, in the number **123**, **1** has the place value of **hundreds**, **2** is **tens**, and **3** is **ones**.

Rectangle. A figure with four corners and four sides. Sides opposite each other are the same length. It looks like this: ▭.

Sequencing. Putting numbers in the correct order, such as 7, 8, 9.

Square. A figure with four corners and four sides of the same length. It looks like this: □.

Subtraction. "Taking away" or subtracting one number from another. For example, 10 - 3 = 7.

Triangle. A figure with three corners and three sides. It looks like this: △.

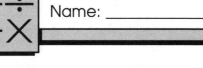

Name: _____

Number Recognition

Directions: Write the numbers 1-10. Color the bear.

Name: _____

Number Recognition 1, 2, 3, 4, 5

Directions: Use the color code to color the parrot.

Color:
1's red
2's blue
3's yellow
4's green
5's orange

Name: _____

Number Recognition 6, 7, 8, 9, 10

Directions: Use the code to color the carousel horse.

Color:
6's purple
7's yellow
8's black
9's pink
10's brown

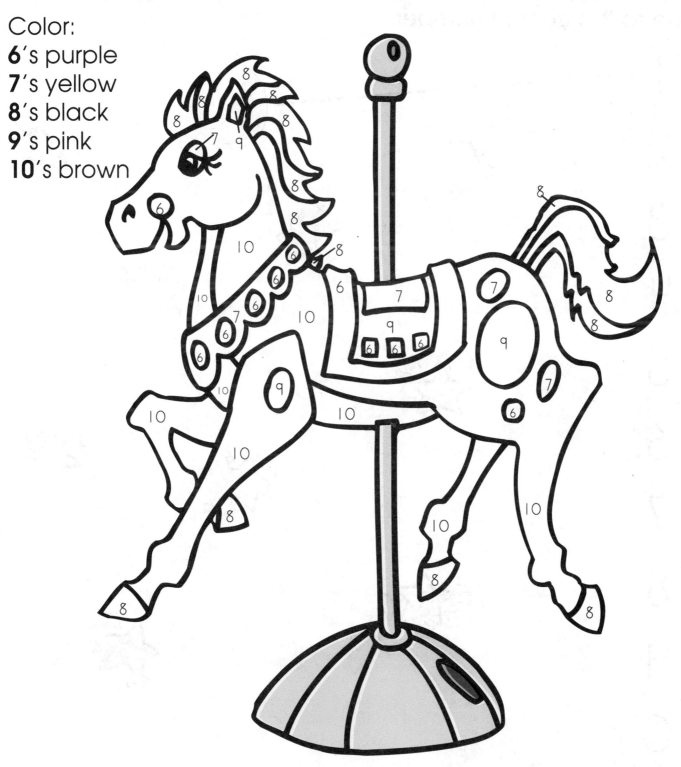

Name: _____

Number Recognition

Directions: Count the number of objects in each group. Draw a line to the correct number.

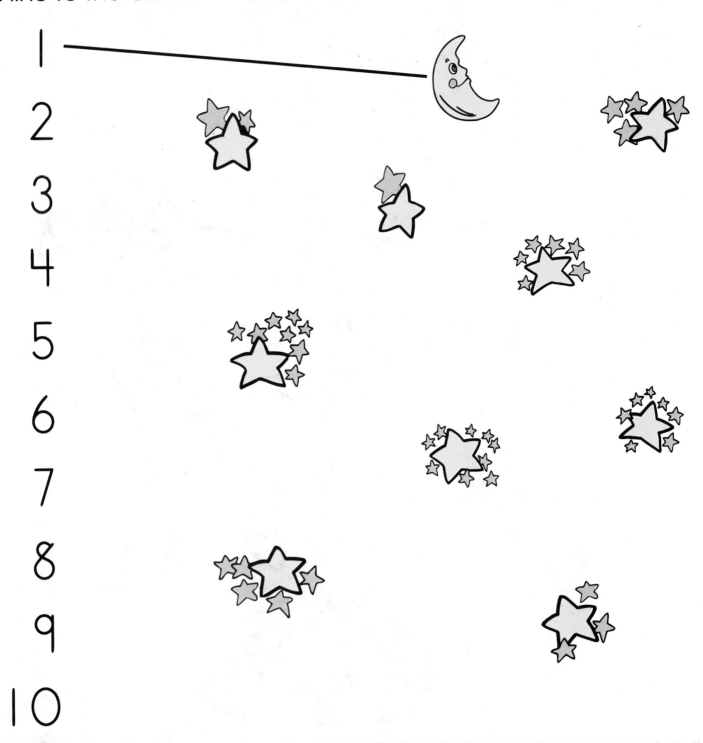

1

2

3

4

5

6

7

8

9

10

Sequencing Numbers

Sequencing is putting numbers in the correct order.

Directions: Write the missing numbers.

Example: 4, ___5___ , 6

3, _____ , 5   7, _____ , 9   8, _____ , 10

6, _____ , 8   _____ , 3, 4   _____ , 5, 6

5, 6, _____   _____ , 6, 7   _____ , 3, 4

_____ , 9, 10   _____ , 7, 8   2, _____ , 4

2, 3, _____   1, 2, _____   7, 8, _____

2, _____ , 4   _____ , 7, 8   4, _____ , 6

6, 7, _____   2, 3, _____   1, _____ , 3

7, 8, _____   _____ , 3, 4   _____ , 9, 10

Name: _____

Counting

Directions: How many are there of each shape? Write the answers in the boxes. The first one is done for you.

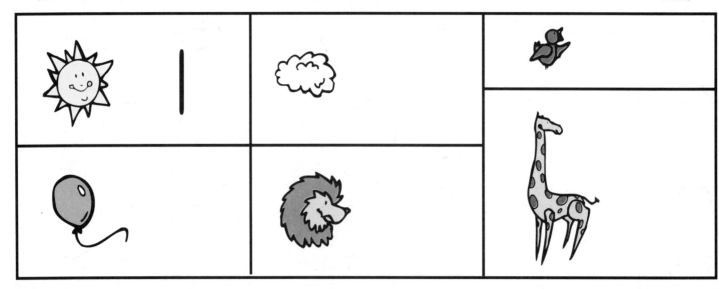

Counting

Directions: How many are there of each shape? Write the answers in the boxes. The first one is done for you.

Name: _____

Review

Directions: Count the shapes and write the answers.

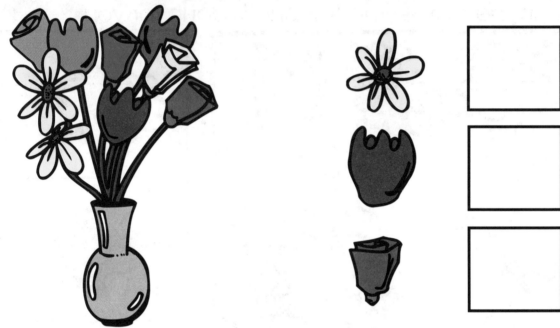

Directions: Fill in the missing numbers. Connect the dots to finish the picture.

Name: _____

Number Words

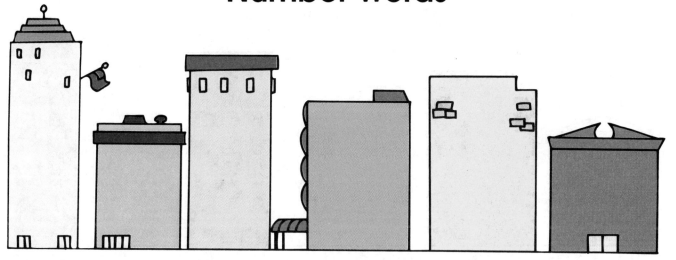

Directions: Number the buildings from one to six.

Directions: Draw a line from the word to the number.

two   1

five   3

six   5

four   6

one   2

three   4

Number Words

Directions: Number the buildings from five to ten.

Directions: Draw a line from the word to the number.

nine   8

seven   10

five   7

eight   5

six   9

ten   6

Name: _____

Shapes: Square

A square is a figure with four corners and four sides of the same length. This is a square □.

Directions: Find the squares and circle them.

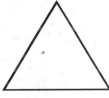

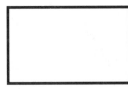

Directions: Trace the word.   Write the word.

square

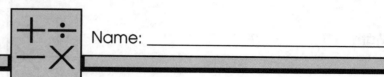

Name: _____

Shapes: Circle

A circle is a figure that is round. This is a circle ○.

Directions: Find the circles and put a square around them.

Directions: Trace the word. Write the word.

circle

Name: _____

Shapes: Triangle

A triangle is a figure with three corners and three sides. This is a triangle △.

Directions: Find the triangles and put a circle around them.

Directions: Trace the word.   Write the word.

triangle

Name: _____

Shapes: Rectangle

A rectangle is a figure with four corners and four sides. Sides opposite each other are the same length. This is a rectangle ▭ .

Directions: Find the rectangles and put a circle around them.

Directions: Trace the word.   Write the word.

rectangle

16

Shapes: Oval And Diamond

An oval is an egg-shaped figure. A diamond is a figure with four sides of the same length. Its corners form points at the top, sides, and bottom. This is an oval⬭. This is a diamond ◇.

Directions: Color the ovals red. Color the diamonds blue.

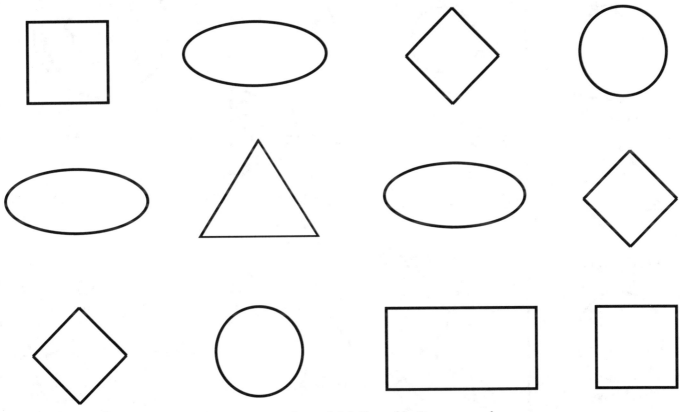

Directions: Trace the words.   Write the words.

oval

diamond

Name: _____

Review

Directions: Color the shapes in the picture as shown.

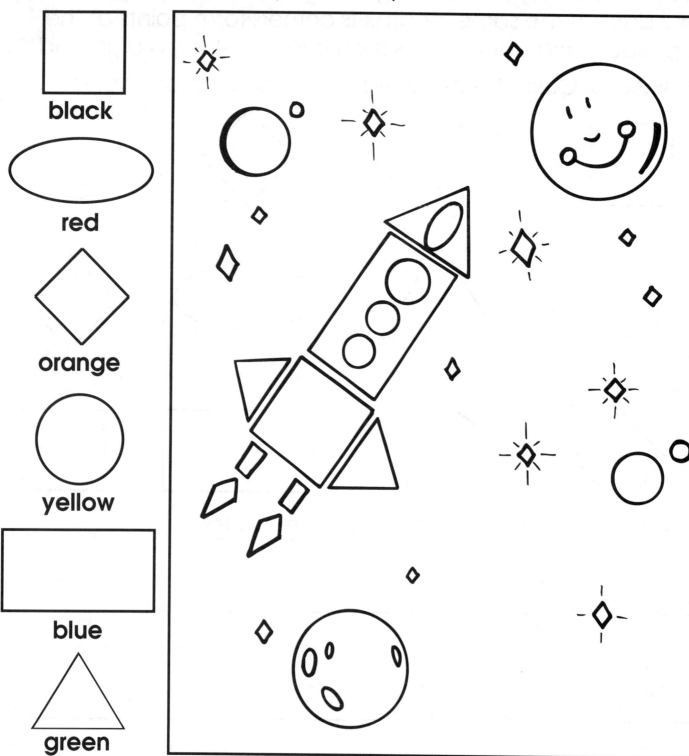

black

red

orange

yellow

blue

green

18

Name: _____

Addition 1, 2

Addition means "putting together" or adding two or more numbers to find the sum.

Directions: Count the cats and tell how many.

 +  =  _____

 = _____

 +  =  _____

Name: _____

Addition 3, 4, 5, 6

Directions: Practice writing the numbers and then add.

3 _____

4 _____

5 _____

6 _____

$$\begin{array}{r} 2 \\ +4 \\ \hline \end{array}$$
$$\begin{array}{r} 1 \\ +4 \\ \hline \end{array}$$

$$\begin{array}{r} 3 \\ +2 \\ \hline \end{array}$$
$$\begin{array}{r} 1 \\ +2 \\ \hline \end{array}$$

Name: _____

Addition 4, 5, 6, 7

Directions: Practice writing the numbers and then add.

4 _____

5 _____

6 _____

7 _____

$$\begin{array}{r} 2 \\ +5 \\ \hline \end{array} \qquad \begin{array}{r} 3 \\ +1 \\ \hline \end{array}$$

$$\begin{array}{r} 4 \\ +1 \\ \hline \end{array} \qquad \begin{array}{r} 2 \\ +4 \\ \hline \end{array}$$

Addition 6, 7, 8

Directions: Practice writing the numbers and then add.

6 _____

7 _____

8 _____

$$\begin{array}{r} 3 \\ +4 \\ \hline \end{array}$$

$$\begin{array}{r} 5 \\ +1 \\ \hline \end{array}$$

$$\begin{array}{r} 2 \\ +6 \\ \hline \end{array}$$

$$\begin{array}{r} 4 \\ +4 \\ \hline \end{array}$$

Addition 7, 8, 9

Directions: Practice writing the numbers and then add.

7   _____

8   _____

9   _____

$$\begin{array}{r} 8 \\ +1 \\ \hline \end{array}$$
$$\begin{array}{r} 3 \\ +5 \\ \hline \end{array}$$

$$\begin{array}{r} 2 \\ +7 \\ \hline \end{array}$$
$$\begin{array}{r} 6 \\ +1 \\ \hline \end{array}$$

Name: ______________________

Subtraction 1, 2, 3

Subtraction means "taking away" or subtracting one number from another.

Directions: Practice writing the numbers and then subtract.

1 ______________________

2 ______________________

3 ______________________

$$\begin{array}{r} 3 \\ -1 \\ \hline \end{array} \qquad \begin{array}{r} 4 \\ -3 \\ \hline \end{array}$$

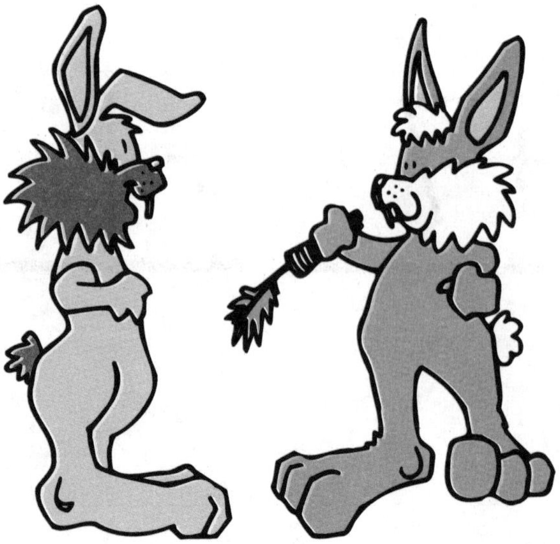

$$\begin{array}{r} 2 \\ -1 \\ \hline \end{array} \qquad \begin{array}{r} 3 \\ -2 \\ \hline \end{array}$$

Name: _____

Subtraction 3, 4, 5, 6

Directions: Practice writing the numbers and then subtract.

3
_____
_____

4
_____
_____

5
_____
_____

6
_____
_____

$$\begin{array}{r} 5 \\ -2 \\ \hline \end{array}$$
$$\begin{array}{r} 6 \\ -1 \\ \hline \end{array}$$

$$\begin{array}{r} 6 \\ -3 \\ \hline \end{array}$$
$$\begin{array}{r} 5 \\ -1 \\ \hline \end{array}$$

25

Name: _____

Review

Directions: Trace the numbers. Work the problems.

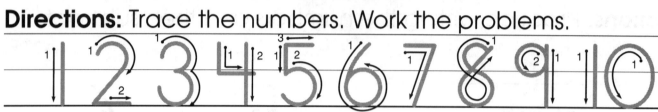

1 2 3 4 5 6 7 8 9 10

$$\begin{array}{r} 9 \\ -3 \\ \hline \end{array}$$

$$\begin{array}{r} 6 \\ +2 \\ \hline \end{array}$$

$$\begin{array}{r} 3 \\ +4 \\ \hline \end{array}$$

$$\begin{array}{r} 2 \\ -1 \\ \hline \end{array}$$

$$\begin{array}{r} 5 \\ +4 \\ \hline \end{array}$$

$$\begin{array}{r} 9 \\ -5 \\ \hline \end{array}$$

$$\begin{array}{r} 7 \\ +2 \\ \hline \end{array}$$

$$\begin{array}{r} 8 \\ -6 \\ \hline \end{array}$$

$$\begin{array}{r} 4 \\ -2 \\ \hline \end{array}$$

$$\begin{array}{r} 6 \\ +3 \\ \hline \end{array}$$

$$\begin{array}{r} 9 \\ -7 \\ \hline \end{array}$$

$$\begin{array}{r} 1 \\ +7 \\ \hline \end{array}$$

Zero

Directions: Write the number.

Example:

How many monkeys?

3

How many monkeys?

0

How many
kites?

How many
kites?

How many flowers?

How many flowers?

How many apples?

How many apples?

Math

Zero

Directions: Write the number that tells how many.

How many sailboats?

_____

How many sailboats?

_____

How many eggs?

_____

How many eggs?

_____

How many marshmallows?

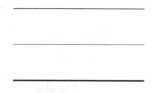

_____

How many marshmallows?

_____

How many candles?

_____

How many candles?

_____

Addition 1, 2, 3, 4, 5

Directions: Add the numbers. Put your answers in the nests.

Example: 2 + 3 =

 1 + 2 =	 1 + 3 =
 4 + 1 =	 1 + 1 =

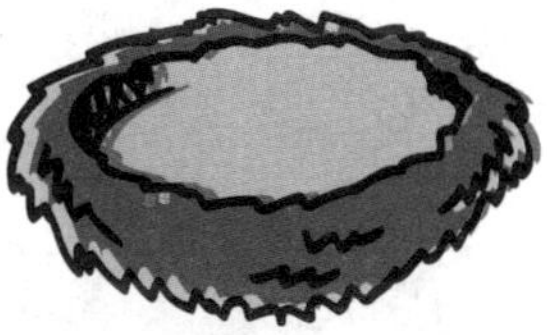

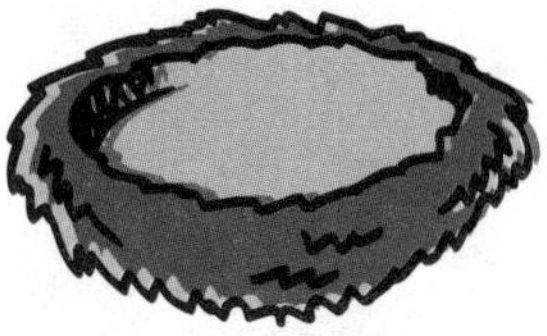

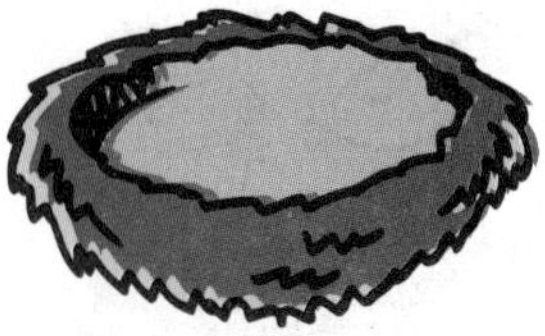

29

Addition 6, 7, 8, 9, 10

Directions: Add the numbers. Put your answers in the doghouses.

Example: $4 + 2 =$

$2 + 6 =$

$7 + 3 =$

$6 + 1 =$

$4 + 5 =$

$6 + 2 =$

$7 + 2 =$

Name: _____

Subtraction 1, 2, 3, 4, 5

Directions: Count the fruit in each bowl. Write your answers on the blanks. Circle the problem that matches your answer.

4

$$\begin{array}{r} 5 \\ -1 \\ \hline \end{array}$$ $$\begin{array}{r} 4 \\ -2 \\ \hline \end{array}$$

_____

$$\begin{array}{r} 3 \\ -0 \\ \hline \end{array}$$ $$\begin{array}{r} 4 \\ -2 \\ \hline \end{array}$$

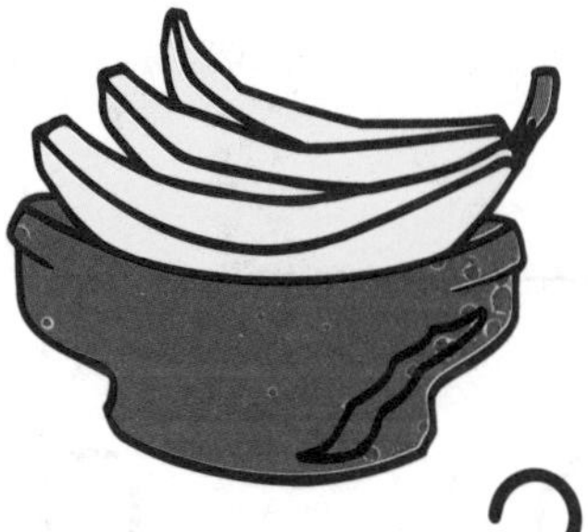

_____

$$\begin{array}{r} 5 \\ -1 \\ \hline \end{array}$$ $$\begin{array}{r} 4 \\ -3 \\ \hline \end{array}$$

_____

$$\begin{array}{r} 3 \\ -2 \\ \hline \end{array}$$ $$\begin{array}{r} 5 \\ -0 \\ \hline \end{array}$$

31

Subtraction 6, 7, 8, 9, 10

Directions: Count the flowers. Write your answers on the blanks. Circle the problems with the same answer.

$$\begin{array}{r}10\\-1\end{array}\qquad\begin{array}{r}9\\-1\end{array}$$

$$\begin{array}{r}7\\-2\end{array}\qquad\begin{array}{r}9\\-3\end{array}$$

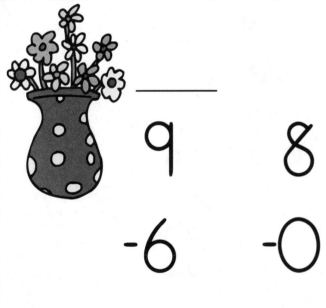

$$\begin{array}{r}9\\-6\end{array}\qquad\begin{array}{r}8\\-0\end{array}$$

$$\begin{array}{r}10\\-2\end{array}\qquad\begin{array}{r}8\\-1\end{array}$$

Addition And Subtraction

Directions: Work the problems. Remember, addition means "putting together" or adding two or more numbers to find the sum. Subtraction means "taking away" or subtracting one number from another.

1 + 3 = _____   4 - 3 = _____   4 + 5 = _____

6 + 1 = _____   7 - 2 = _____   8 - 4 = _____

                     9 - 1 = _____   10 - 3 = _____

                     5 - 2 = _____   6 + 3 = _____

                     8 + 2 = _____   5 + 5 = _____

Math

Review

Directions: Work the problems. Color the picture.

Place Value: Tens And Ones

The place value of a digit, or numeral, is shown by where it is in the number. For example, in the number **123**, **1** has the place value of **hundreds**, **2** is **tens**, and **3** is **ones**.

Directions: Count the groups of ten crayons and write the number by the word **tens**. Count the other crayons and write the number by the word **ones**.

Example:  + = __|__ ten + __|__ one

 + = ____ tens + ____ ones

 + = ____ tens + ____ ones

 + = ____ tens + ____ ones

6 tens + 3 ones = ____   5 tens + 1 one = ____

3 tens + 8 ones = ____   9 tens + 7 ones = ____

4 tens + 5 ones = ____   2 tens + 8 ones = ____

Name: _____

Place Value: Tens And Ones

Directions: Write the answers in the correct spaces.

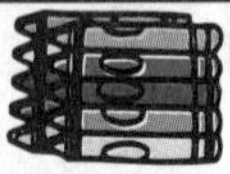

		tens	ones		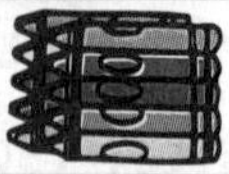 
3 tens, 2 ones		_3_	_2_	=	_32_
3 tens, 7 ones		___	___	=	___
9 tens, 1 one		___	___	=	___
5 tens, 6 ones		___	___	=	___
6 tens, 5 ones		___	___	=	___
6 tens, 8 ones		___	___	=	___
2 tens, 8 ones		___	___	=	___
4 tens, 9 ones		___	___	=	___
1 ten, 4 ones		___	___	=	___
8 tens, 2 ones		___	___	=	___
4 tens, 2 ones		___	___	=	___

28 = ____ tens, ____ ones

64 = ____ tens, ____ ones

56 = ____ tens, ____ ones

72 = ____ tens, ____ ones

38 = ____ tens, ____ ones

17 = ____ tens, ____ ones

63 = ____ tens, ____ ones

12 = ____ tens, ____ ones

Name: _____

Ordinal Numbers

Ordinal numbers are used to indicate order in a series, such as **first**, **second**, or **third**.

Directions: Draw a line to the picture that corresponds to the ordinal number in the left column.

eighth

third

sixth

ninth

seventh

second

fourth

first

fifth

tenth

37

Name: _____

Counting By Tens

Directions: Count in order by tens to draw the path the boy takes to the store.

Counting By Fives

Directions: Count by fives to draw the path to the playground.

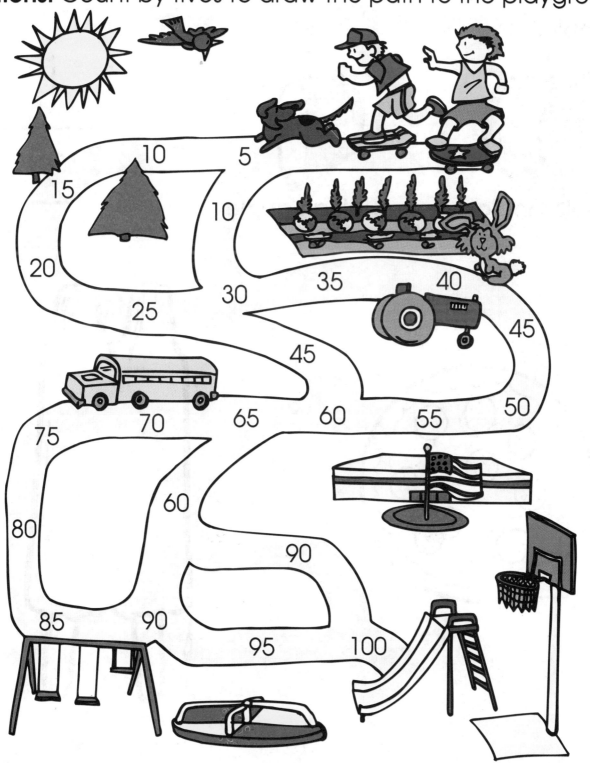

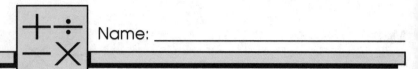

Fractions: Whole And Half

Directions: Color half of each object.

Example:

Whole apple

Half an apple

$$\frac{1}{2}$$

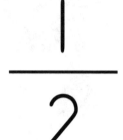
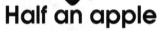

Name: _____

Fractions: Thirds And Fourths

A fraction is a number that names part of a whole, such as **1/2** or **3/4**.

Directions: Each object has 3 equal parts. Color one section.

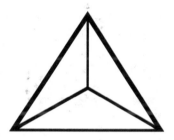  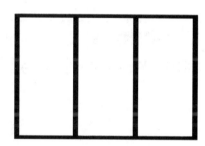

Directions: Each object has 4 equal parts. Color one section.

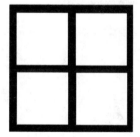  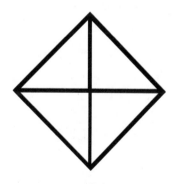

Name: _____

Review

Directions: Write the missing numbers by counting by tens and fives.

____ , 20, ____ , ____ , ____ , ____ , 70, ____ , ____ , 100

5, ____ , 15, ____ , ____ , 30, ____ , ____ , ____ , ____

Directions: Color the object with thirds red. Color the object with halves blue. Color the object with fourths green.

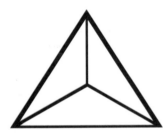  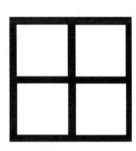

Directions: Draw a line to the correct equal part.

$\dfrac{1}{3}$

$\dfrac{1}{4}$

$\dfrac{1}{2}$

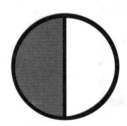

Name: _____

Addition: 10 - 15

Directions: Circle groups of ten crayons. Add the remaining ones to make the correct number.

			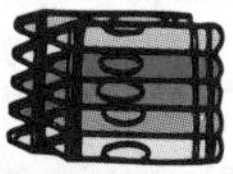  tens	ones
	+	=	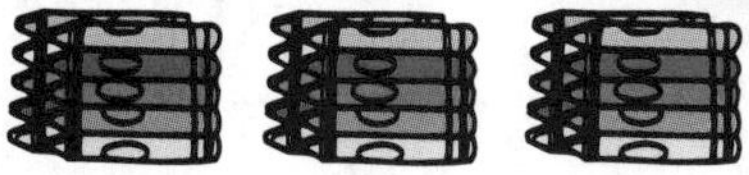 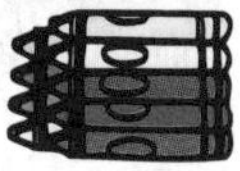 3	9
	+	=		
	+	=		
	+	=		
	+	=		
	+	=		

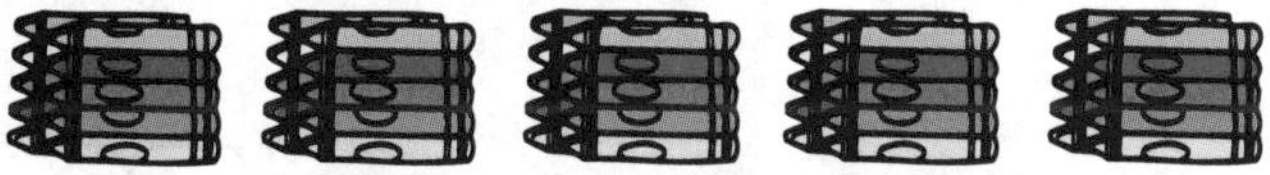

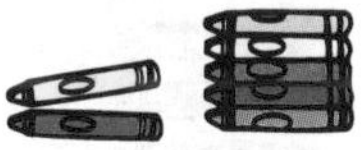

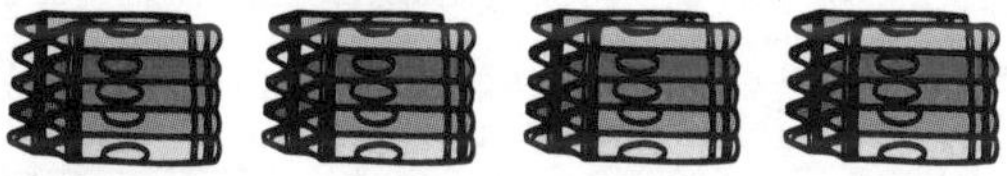

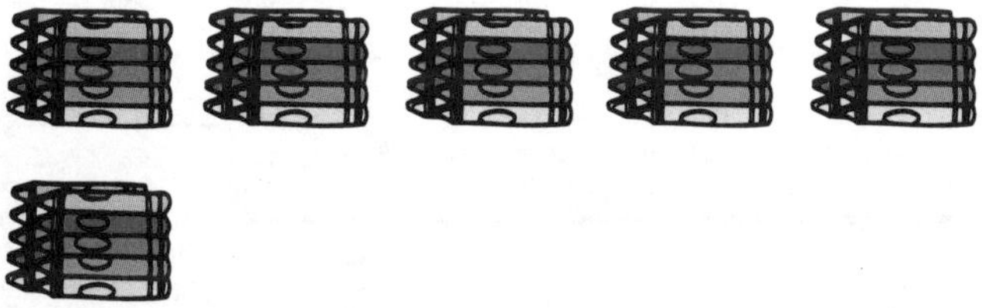

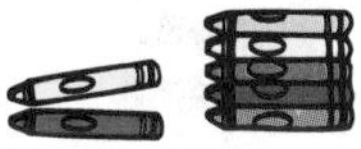

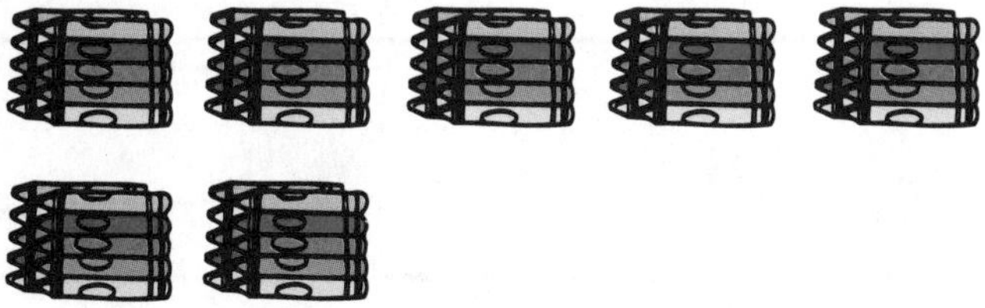

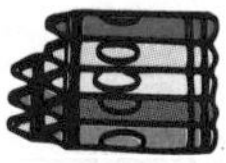

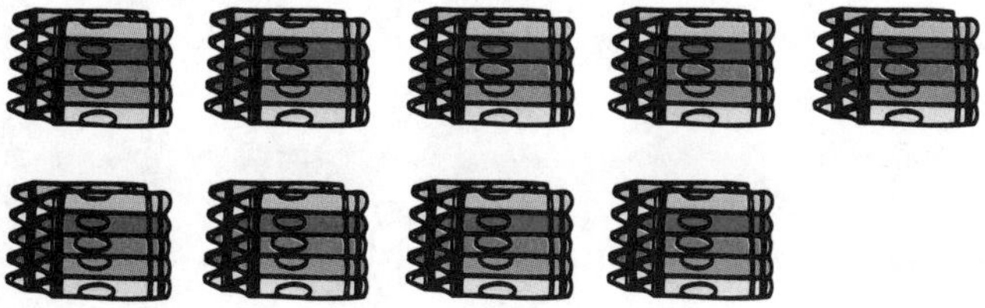

6 + 6 = _____   8 + 4 = _____   9 + 5 = _____

Name: _____

Subtraction: 10 - 15

Directions: Count the crayons in each group. Put an **X** through the number of crayons being subtracted. How many are left?

		-	5	=	<u>10</u>

 - 4 = _____

  - 7 = _____

  - 6 = _____

 - 5 = _____

  - 8 = _____

13 - 8 = _____	11 - 5 = _____	12 - 9 = _____
14 - 7 = _____	10 - 7 = _____	13 - 3 = _____
15 - 9 = _____	11 - 8 = _____	12 - 10 = _____

Name: _____

Addition And Subtraction

Remember, addition means "putting together" or adding two or more numbers to find the sum. Subtraction means "taking away" or subtracting one number from another.

Directions: Work the problems. From your answers, use the code to color the quilt.

Color:

6 = blue
7 = yellow
8 = green
9 = red
10 = orange

Time: Hour

The short hand of the clock tells the hour. The long hand tells how many minutes after the hour. When the minute hand is on the **12**, it is the beginning of the hour.

Directions: Look at each clock. Write the time.

Example:

___3___ o'clock

____ o'clock

____ o'clock

____ o'clock

____ o'clock

____ o'clock

____ o'clock

____ o'clock

____ o'clock

Time: Hour, Half-Hour

The short hand of the clock tells the hour. The long hand tells how many minutes after the hour. When the minute hand is on the **6**, it is on the half-hour. A half-hour is thirty minutes. It is written **:30**, such as **5:30**.

Directions: Look at each clock. Write the time.

Example:

hour   half-hour

__1__ : __30__

____ : ____ ____ : ____ ____ : ____ ____ : ____

____ : ____ ____ : ____ ____ : ____ ____ : ____

Math

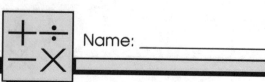

Name: _____

Time: Hour, Half-Hour

Directions: Draw the hands on each clock to show the correct time.

   **2:30**

   **9:00**

   **7:00**

   **4:30**

   **3:00**

   **1:30**

Money: Penny And Nickel

A penny is worth one cent. It is written **1¢** or **$.01**. A nickel is worth five cents. It is written **5¢** or **$.05**.

Directions: Count the money and write the answers.

penny   1 penny = 1¢

nickel   1 nickel = 5¢

= ___3___ ¢

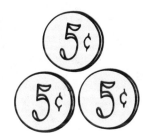

= ___15___ ¢

= _____ ¢

= _____ ¢

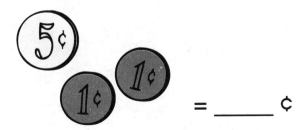

= _____ ¢

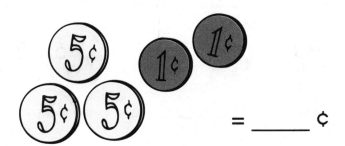

= _____ ¢

Name: _____

Review

Directions: What time is it?

_____ o'clock

Directions: Draw the hands on each clock.

2:30

7:30

11:00

Directions: How much money?

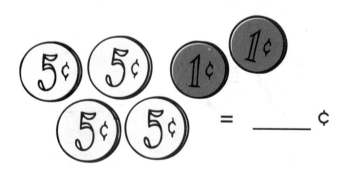

= _____ ¢

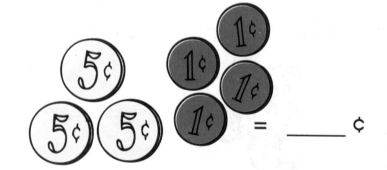

= _____ ¢

Directions: Add or Subtract.

$9 + 3 =$ _____ $\qquad$ $6 + 8 =$ _____ $\qquad$ $15 - 9 =$ _____

$13 - 8 =$ _____ $\qquad$ $12 + 2 =$ _____ $\qquad$ $7 + 6 =$ _____

Name: _____

Picture Problems: Addition 0 - 9

Directions: Work the number problem under each picture.

6 + 2 = _____

3 + 1 = _____

5 + 3 = _____

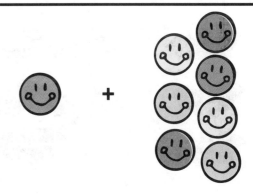

1 + 7 = _____

4 + 5 = _____

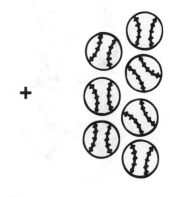

0 + 7 = _____

Name: _____

Picture Problems: Addition 0 - 9

Directions: Work the number problem under each picture.

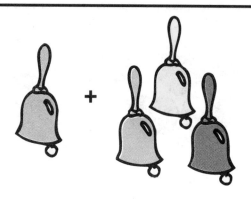

1 + 3 = _____

2 + 4 = _____

3 + 5 = _____

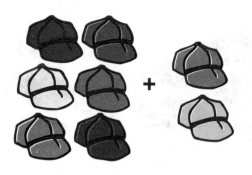

6 + 2 = _____

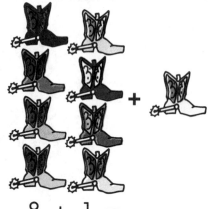

8 + 1 = _____

0 + 7 = _____

Name: _____

Picture Problems: Subtraction

Directions: Work the number problem under each picture.

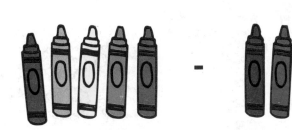

5 - 2 = _____

6 - 1 = _____

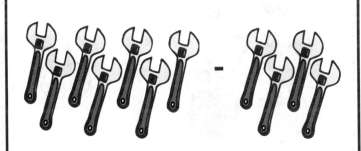

7 - 4 = _____

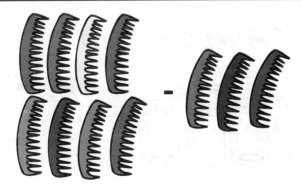

8 - 3 = _____

9 - 2 = _____

4 - 4 = _____

Name: _____

Picture Problems: Subtraction

Directions: Work the number problem under each picture.

6 - 2 = _____

9 - 5 = _____

7 - 2 = _____

4 - 1 = _____

8 - 1 = _____

4 - 0 = _____

Name: _____

Picture Problems: Addition And Subtraction

Directions: Work the number problem under each picture.

7 - 4 = _____

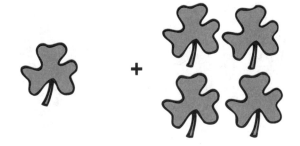

1 + 4 = _____

3 + 5 = _____

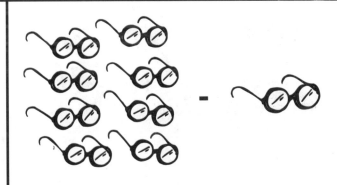

8 - 1 = _____

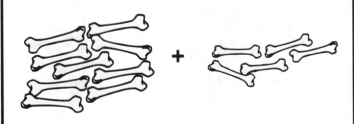

9 + 5 = _____

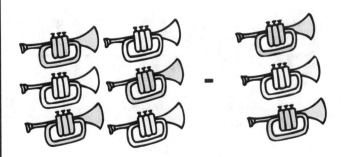

6 - 3 = _____

Name: _____

Picture Problems: Addition and Subtraction

Directions: Work the number problem under each picture.
Write **+** or **-** to show if you should add or subtract.

How many 's in all?

$4 + 5 =$ ___9___

How many 's in all?

$7 \quad 5 =$ _____

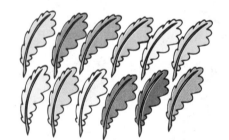 

How many 's are left?

$12 \quad 3 =$ _____

How many 's are left?

$15 \quad 8 =$ _____

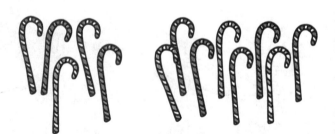

How many 's in all?

$5 \quad 8 =$ _____

How many 's are left?

$11 \quad 4 =$ _____

Name: _____

Picture Problems: Addition and Subtraction

Directions: Work the number problem under each picture.
Write **+** or **-** to show if you should add or subtract.

How many 's in all?

7 **+** 5 = __12__

How many 's are left?

8   3 = _____

How many 's are left?

9   4 = _____

How many 's in all?

14   1 = _____

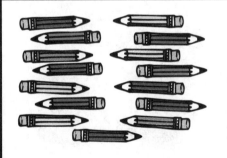 

How many 's are left?

15   6 = _____

How many 's in all?

9   5 = _____

Review

Directions: Work the number problem under each picture.
Write **+** or **-** to show if you should add or subtract.

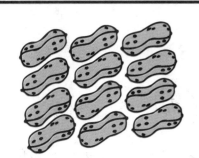 

How many 's are left?

12 ____ 4 = ____

How many 's in all?

6 ____ 8 = ____

How many 's are left?

4 ____ 4 = ____

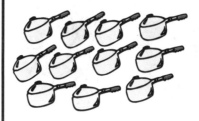

How many 's are left?

11 ____ 7 = ____

How many 's in all?

9 ____ 3 = ____

How many 's in all?

10 ____ 0 = ____

Name: _____

Money: Penny, Nickel, Dime

A penny is worth one cent. It is written **1¢** or **$.01**. A nickel is worth five cents. It is written **5¢** or **$.05**. A dime is worth ten cents. It is written **10¢** or **$.10**.

Directions: Add the coins pictured and write the total amounts in the blanks.

Example:

   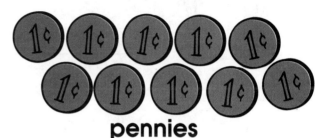

dime	 nickel	 nickel	pennies
10¢ =	5¢ +	5¢ =	10¢

10¢   +   1¢     =   _____ ¢   10¢   + _____ ¢ = _____ ¢

_____   +   _____   +   _____   =   _____ ¢

_____ ¢ =   _____ ¢   =   _____ ¢

Time: Hour, Half-Hour

Directions: Tell what time it is on the clocks.

 _____

 _____

 _____

 _____

 _____

 _____

Name: _____

Shapes: Square, Circle, Rectangle, Triangle

Directions: Use the code to color the shapes.

Squares - Orange
Circles - Red
Rectangles - Blue
Triangles - Green

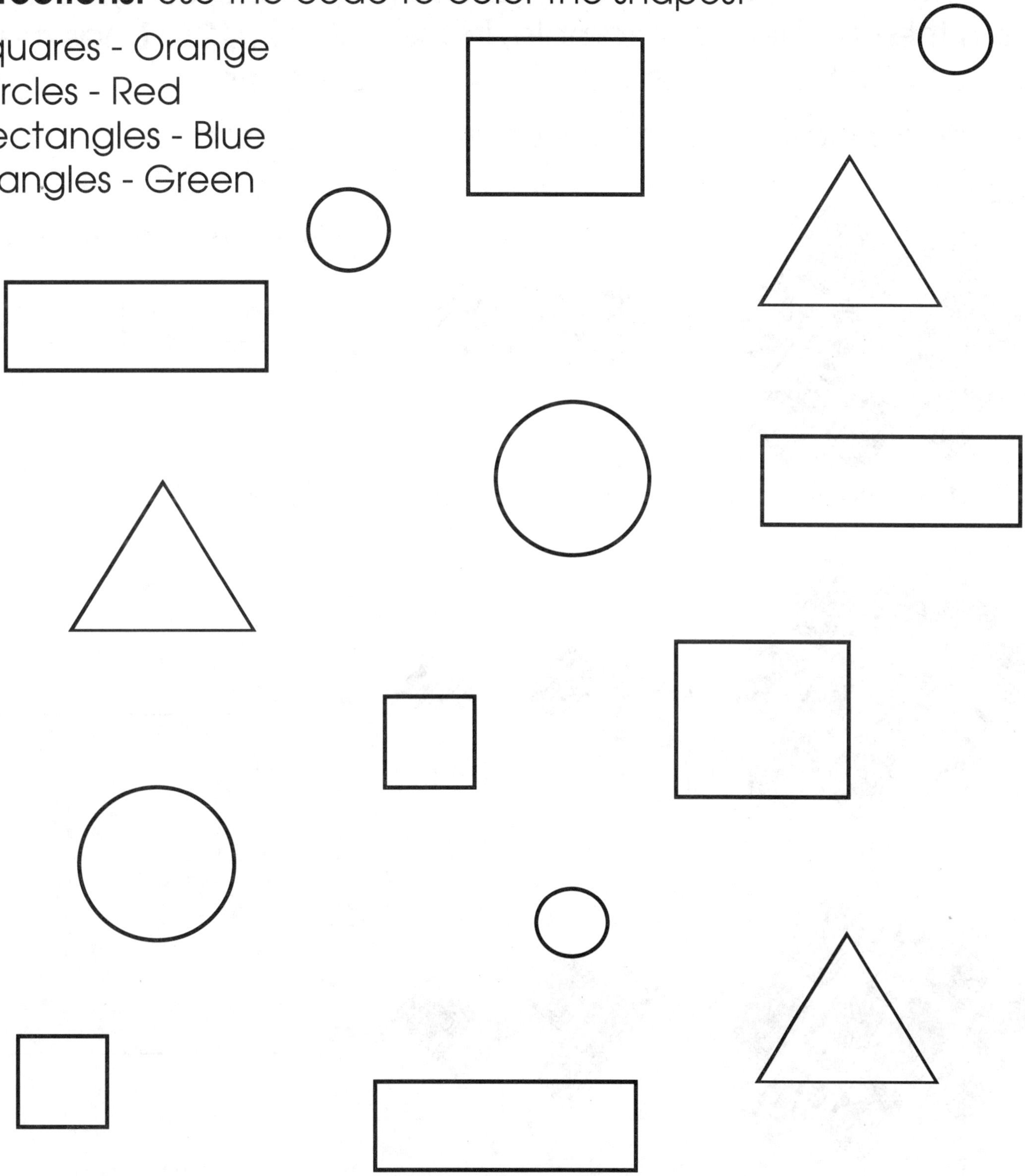

Name: _____

Place Value: Tens, Ones And One Hundred

The place value of each digit, or numeral, is shown by where it is in the number. For example, in the number **123**, **1** has the place value of **hundreds**, **2** is **tens**, and **3** is **ones**.

Directions: Count the groups of crayons and add.

Example:

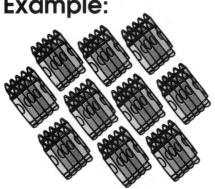

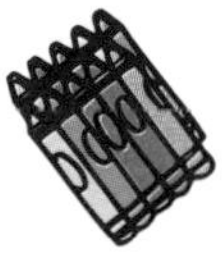

	Hundreds	Tens	Ones
=	1	1	3

1 Hundred + 1 Ten + 3 Ones

= _____ _____ _____

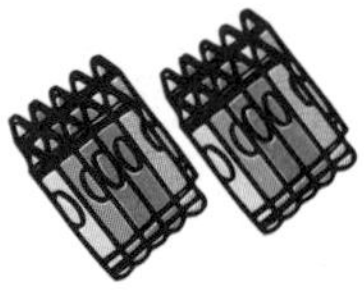

= _____ _____ _____

Name: _____

Fractions: Half, Third, Fourth

Directions: Count the equal parts, then write the fraction.

Example:

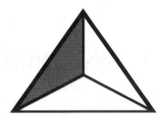

Shaded part = __1__   Write $\dfrac{1}{3}$

Equal parts = __3__

Shaded part = __1__   Write

Equal parts = _____ $\dfrac{}{}$

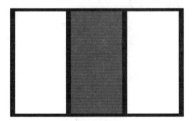

Shaded part = __1__   Write

Equal parts = _____ $\dfrac{}{}$

Shaded part = __1__   Write

Equal parts = _____ $\dfrac{}{}$

Name: _____

Review

Directions: Follow the instructions.

1. How much money?

    _____ ¢

	Tens	Ones		Hundreds	Tens	Ones
2. 57 =	_____	_____	128 =	_____	_____	_____

3. What is this shape? Circle the answer.

Square
Triangle
Circle

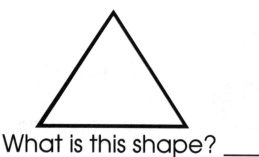
What is this shape? _____

4.    Shaded part = _____   Write

Equal parts = _____   ‾‾‾

   Shaded part = _____   Write

Equal parts = _____   ‾‾‾

5. 12 + 3 = _____   9 + 6 = _____   15 - 7 = _____

My Name

Do this with a grown-up.

My first name is _____ .

My first name has _____ letters.

My last name is _____ .

My last name has _____ letters.
Count these letters in your name.

a ____   **e** ____   **i** ____   **o** ____   **u** ____

Color a box for each **a**, **e**, **i**, **o**, and **u** in your name.

7	7	7	7	7
6	6	6	6	6
5	5	5	5	5
4	4	4	4	4
3	3	3	3	3
2	2	2	2	2
1	1	1	1	1
a	**e**	**i**	**o**	**u**

Which has more?   **a   e   i   o   u**

Counting, Graphing, and Comparing Numbers

Fill the Spoon

Play this with a grown-up.

You need a tablespoon.

You need a box or jar of little things, like dried beans, nuts or popcorn.

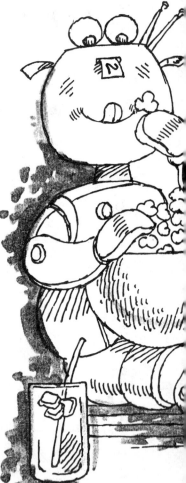

Fill the spoon with beans.

Guess how many. _____

Count how many. _____

Fill the spoon again. Try to put in even more!

Guess how many. _____

Count how many. _____

Estimating and Counting

Name Writing Contest

Do this with a grown-up.

Color the boxes with these numbers: 5, 10, 15, 20, 25, 30, 35, 40, 45, 50, 55, 60, 65, 70, 75, 80, 85, 90, 95, 100.

1	2	3	4	5	6	7	8	9	10
11	12	13	14	15	16	17	18	19	20
21	22	23	24	25	26	27	28	29	30
31	32	33	34	35	36	37	38	39	40
41	42	43	44	45	46	47	48	49	50
51	52	53	54	55	56	57	58	59	60
61	62	63	64	65	66	67	68	69	70
71	72	73	74	75	76	77	78	79	80
81	82	83	84	85	86	87	88	89	90
91	92	93	94	95	96	97	98	99	100

Do you see a pattern? _____

Have your grown-up count by fives to 100.

Write your name as often as you can while he counts.

How many times did you write your name? _____

Count Up Time

Ask a grown-up to help you.

You need many things like dried beans or paper clips.

1	2	3	4	5	6
7	8	9	10	11	12

Put 1 bean in box 1.

Put 2 beans in box 2.

Put 3 beans in box 3, and so on up to box 12.

Count all the beans. How many in all? _____

Counting to 78

Circle Them Up

Do this with a grown-up.

You need some little things, like dried beans or paper clips.

Count 19 beans.

Put 4 beans in each circle. Put the left-over beans in the triangle.

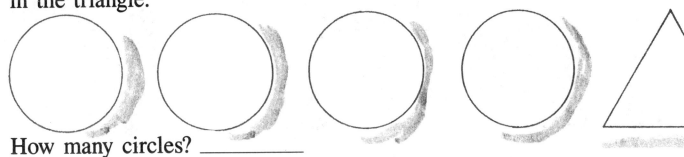

How many circles? _____

How many beans are in the triangle? _____

Do it again. This time put 10 beans in the circle.
Put the left-over beans in the triangle.

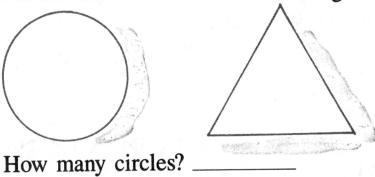

How many circles? _____

How many beans are in the triangle? _____

Grouping Numbers

What's Hiding?

Play this game with a grown-up.

You need 10 little things like beans, pennies, or paper clips.

Step 1 The grown-up puts some on a table. You count how many.

Step 2 Close your eyes. The grown-up takes some away.

Step 3 You open your eyes. Count how many are left.

Step 4 Tell how many are missing.

If you are right, you color a circle.
If you are wrong, the grown-up colors a circle.

Your circles: ◯ ◯ ◯ ◯ ◯ ◯

The grown-up's circles: ◯ ◯ ◯ ◯ ◯ ◯

Subtracting with Basic Facts

Lose and Win Game

Play this game with a grown-up.

You need **20** pennies or paper clips.

You take 10 and your grown-up takes 10.

You also need something **VERY** small, like a bean.

Here is the game board.

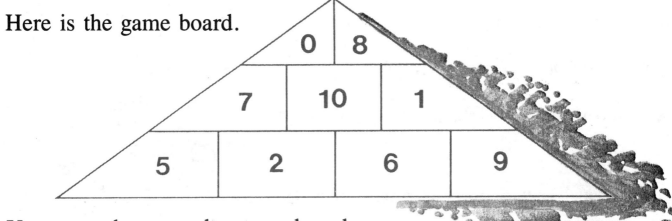

You toss a bean on the game board.

What number did you get? _____

Take away that many pennies from your penny pile.

How many pennies do you have left? _____

Your grown-up tosses a bean.

What number did your grown-up get? _____

Your grown-up takes away that many pennies.

How many pennies does your grown-up have
left? _____

Who has more pennies now? _____   Hooray, the
winner!

Play again. Who is the winner? _____

Tic-Tac-Toe

Play these tic-tac-toe games with a grown-up.

Play them just like all tic-tac-toe games.

Before you mark **X** or **O**, you must add or subtract.

If your answer is right, put your mark in the box.

If your answer is wrong, try again.

When you get the right answer, put your mark in the box.

Take turns. Try to mark **3** boxes in a row.

8 – 5	6 + 6	3 + 8
6 + 7	8 – 3	13 – 3
3 + 2	9 + 1	5 + 8

8 + 9	6 – 2	12 – 3
8 + 4	8 + 8	7 – 3
12 – 4	8 – 4	8 + 10

10 – 3	11 – 3	6 + 4
11 – 4	10 + 5	15 – 5
13 + 2	10 – 4	13 – 3

ANSWER KEY

MASTER MATH
1

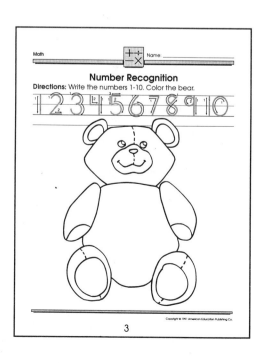

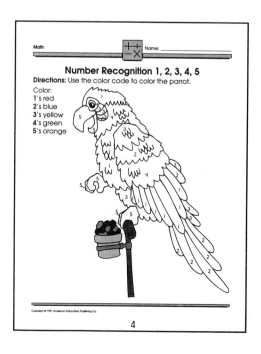

Number Recognition 6, 7, 8, 9, 10

Directions: Use the code to color the carousel horse.

Color:
6's purple
7's yellow
8's black
9's pink
10's brown

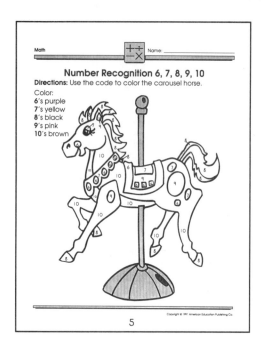

5

Counting

Directions: How many are there of each? Write the answers in the boxes. The first one is done for you.

☀	1	☁	7	🍂	6
🎈	10	🦁	3	🦒	2

8

Number Recognition

Directions: Count the number of objects in each group. Draw a line to the correct number.

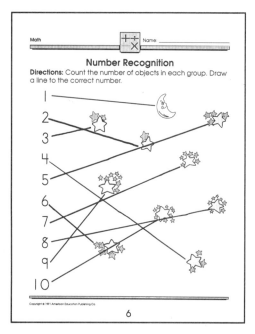

1
2
3
4
5
6
7
8
9
10

6

Counting

Directions: How many are there of each? Write the answers in the boxes. The first one is done for you.

☁	7
🐸	4
🍎	10
🍃	5
🐦	3

9

Sequencing Numbers

Sequencing is putting numbers in the correct order.
Directions: Write the missing numbers.

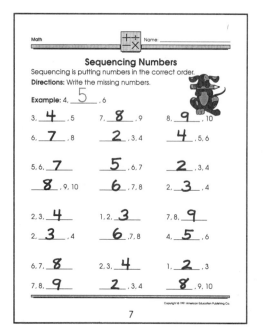

Example: 4, __5__, 6

3, __4__, 5   7, __8__, 9   8, __9__, 10

6, __7__, 8   __2__, 3, 4   __4__, 5, 6

5, 6, __7__   __5__, 6, 7   __2__, 3, 4

__8__, 9, 10   __6__, 7, 8   2, __3__, 4

2, 3, __4__   1, 2, __3__   7, 8, __9__

2, __3__, 4   __6__, 7, 8   __5__, 6

6, 7, __8__   2, __4__   1, __2__, 3

7, 8, __9__   __2__, 3, 4   __8__, 9, 10

7

74

Review

Directions: Count the shapes and write the answers.

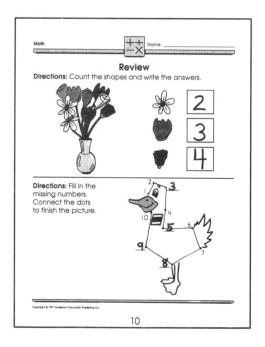

2
3
4

Directions: Fill in the missing numbers. Connect the dots to finish the picture.

10

Number Words

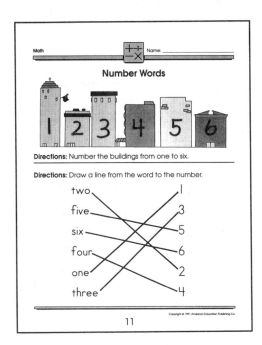

Directions: Number the buildings from one to six.

Directions: Draw a line from the word to the number.

two   1
five   3
six   5
four   6
one   2
three   4

11

Number Words

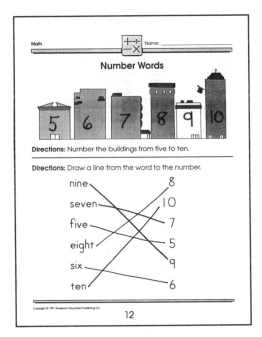

Directions: Number the buildings from five to ten.

Directions: Draw a line from the word to the number.

nine   8
seven   10
five   7
eight   5
six   9
ten   6

12

Shapes: Square

A square is a figure with four corners and four sides of the same length. This is a square ☐.

Directions: Find the squares and circle them.

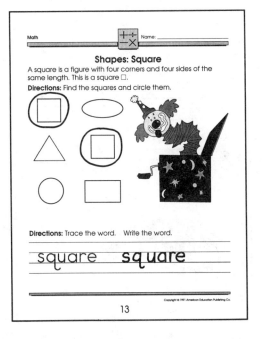

Directions: Trace the word. Write the word.

square   square

13

Shapes: Circle

A circle is a figure that is round. This is a circle ○.

Directions: Find the circles and put a square around them.

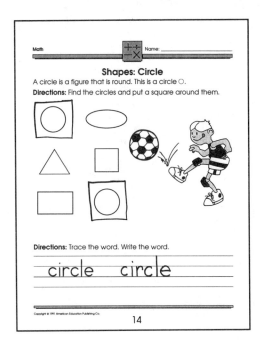

Directions: Trace the word. Write the word.

circle   circle

14

Shapes: Triangle

A triangle is a figure with three corners and three sides. This is a triangle △.

Directions: Find the triangles and put a circle around them.

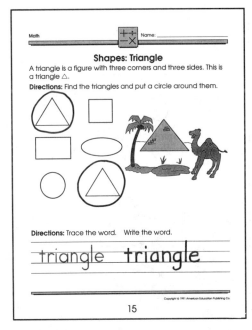

Directions: Trace the word. Write the word.

triangle   triangle

15

Shapes: Rectangle

A rectangle is a figure with four corners and four sides. Sides opposite each other are the same length. This is a rectangle ☐.

Directions: Find the rectangles and put a circle around them.

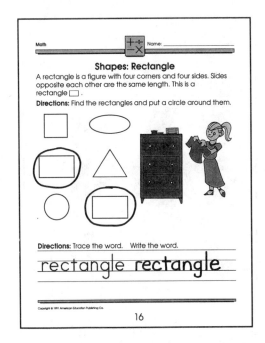

Directions: Trace the word. Write the word.

rectangle   rectangle

16

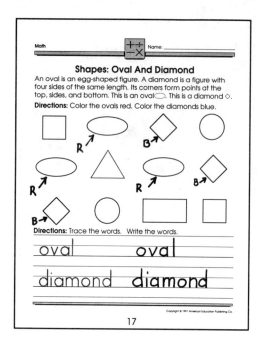

Shapes: Oval And Diamond

An oval is an egg-shaped figure. A diamond is a figure with four sides of the same length. Its corners form points at the top, sides, and bottom. This is an oval ⬭. This is a diamond ◇.

Directions: Color the ovals red. Color the diamonds blue.

Directions: Trace the words. Write the words.

oval   oval

diamond   diamond

17

Addition 3, 4, 5, 6

Directions: Practice writing the numbers and then add.

3 3
4 4
5 5
6 6

$$\begin{array}{r} 2 \\ +4 \\ \hline 6 \end{array} \qquad \begin{array}{r} 1 \\ +4 \\ \hline 5 \end{array}$$

$$\begin{array}{r} 3 \\ +2 \\ \hline 5 \end{array} \qquad \begin{array}{r} 1 \\ +2 \\ \hline 3 \end{array}$$

20

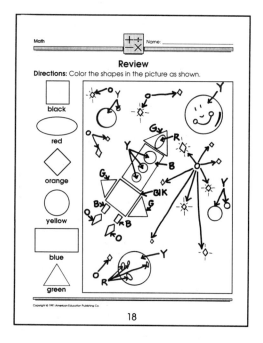

Review

Directions: Color the shapes in the picture as shown.

black
red
orange
yellow
blue
green

18

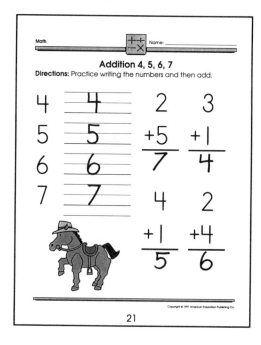

Addition 4, 5, 6, 7

Directions: Practice writing the numbers and then add.

4 4
5 5
6 6
7 7

$$\begin{array}{r} 2 \\ +5 \\ \hline 7 \end{array} \qquad \begin{array}{r} 3 \\ +1 \\ \hline 4 \end{array}$$

$$\begin{array}{r} 4 \\ +1 \\ \hline 5 \end{array} \qquad \begin{array}{r} 2 \\ +4 \\ \hline 6 \end{array}$$

21

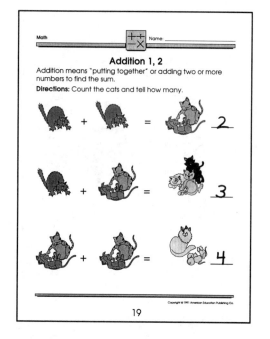

Addition 1, 2

Addition means "putting together" or adding two or more numbers to find the sum.

Directions: Count the cats and tell how many.

+ = 2

+ = 3

+ = 4

19

76

Addition 6, 7, 8

Directions: Practice writing the numbers and then add.

6 6
7 7
8 8

$$\begin{array}{r} 3 \\ +4 \\ \hline 7 \end{array} \qquad \begin{array}{r} 5 \\ +1 \\ \hline 6 \end{array}$$

$$\begin{array}{r} 2 \\ +6 \\ \hline 8 \end{array} \qquad \begin{array}{r} 4 \\ +4 \\ \hline 8 \end{array}$$

22

Addition 7, 8, 9
Directions: Practice writing the numbers and then add.

7   7   8   3

8   8   +1   +5

9   9   9   8

        2   6

     +7   +1

      9   7

23

Subtraction
Subtraction means "taking away" or subtracting one number from another.

Directions: Practice writing the numbers and then subtract.

1   1   3   4

2   2   -1   -3

3   3   2   1

        2   3

     -1   -2

      1   1

24

Subtraction 3, 4, 5, 6
Directions: Practice writing the numbers and then subtract.

3   3   5   6

4   4   -2   -1

5   5   3   5

6   6   6   5

     -3   -1

      3   4

25

Review
Directions: Trace the numbers. Work the problems.

1 2 3 4 5 6 7 8 9 10

9   6   3   2

-3   +2   +4   -1

6   8   7   1

5   9   7   8

+4   -5   +2   -6

9   4   9   2

4   6   9   1

-2   +3   -7   +7

2   9   2   8

26

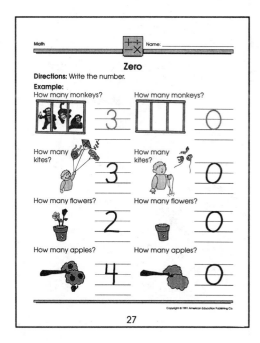

Zero
Directions: Write the number.

Example:

How many monkeys?   How many monkeys?

3   0

How many kites?   How many kites?

3   0

How many flowers?   How many flowers?

2   0

How many apples?   How many apples?

4   0

27

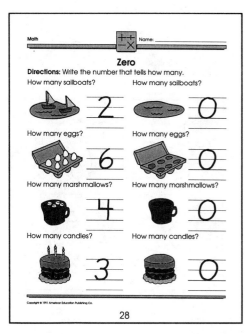

Zero
Directions: Write the number that tells how many.

How many sailboats?   How many sailboats?

2   0

How many eggs?   How many eggs?

6   0

How many marshmallows?   How many marshmallows?

4   0

How many candles?   How many candles?

3   0

28

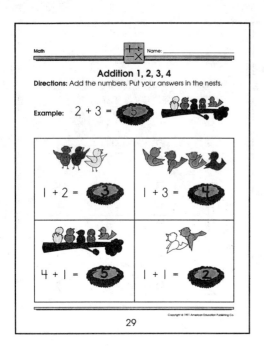

Math Name: _____

Addition 1, 2, 3, 4
Directions: Add the numbers. Put your answers in the nests.

Example: 2 + 3 = 5

1 + 2 = 3   1 + 3 = 4

4 + 1 = 5   1 + 1 = 2

29

Math Name: _____

Addition 6, 7, 8, 9, 10
Directions: Add the numbers. Put your answers in the doghouses.

Example: 4 + 2 = 6

2 + 6 = 8   7 + 3 = 10

6 + 1 = 7   4 + 5 = 9

6 + 2 = 8   7 + 2 = 9

30

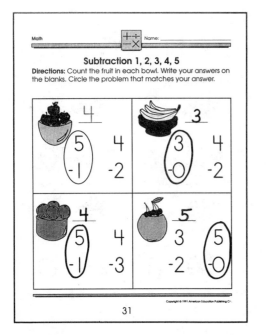

Math Name: _____

Subtraction 1, 2, 3, 4, 5
Directions: Count the fruit in each bowl. Write your answers on the blanks. Circle the problem that matches your answer.

4
5   4
-1   -2

3
3   4
-0   -2

4
5   4
-1   -3

5
3   5
-2   -0

31

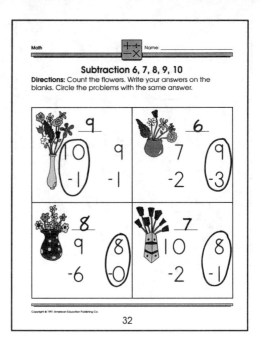

Math Name: _____

Subtraction 6, 7, 8, 9, 10
Directions: Count the flowers. Write your answers on the blanks. Circle the problems with the same answer.

9
10   9
-1   -1

6
7   9
-2   -3

8
9   8
-6   -0

7
10   8
-2   -1

32

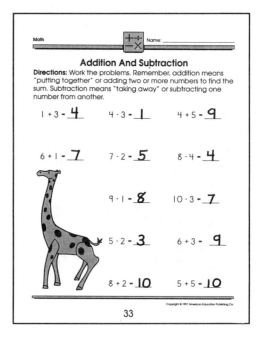

Math Name: _____

Addition And Subtraction
Directions: Work the problems. Remember, addition means "putting together" or adding two or more numbers to find the sum. Subtraction means "taking away" or subtracting one number from another.

1 + 3 - 4   4 - 3 - 1   4 + 5 - 9

6 + 1 - 7   7 - 2 - 5   8 - 4 - 4

9 - 1 - 8   10 - 3 - 7

5 - 2 - 3   6 + 3 - 9

8 + 2 - 10   5 + 5 - 10

33

Math Name: _____

Review
Directions: Work the problems. Color the picture.

5 - 4 = 1   9 + 1 = 10

34

78

Place Value: Tens And Ones

The place value of a digit, or numeral, is shown by where it is in the number. For example, in the number **123**, **1** has the place value of **hundreds**, **2** is **tens**, and **3** is **ones**.

Directions: Count the groups of ten crayons and write the number by the word **tens**. Count the other crayons and write the number by the word **ones**.

Example:

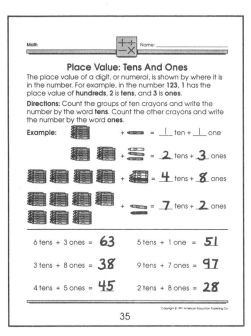

6 tens + 3 ones = **63**   5 tens + 1 one = **51**

3 tens + 8 ones = **38**   9 tens + 7 ones = **97**

4 tens + 5 ones = **45**   2 tens + 8 ones = **28**

35

Counting By Tens

Directions: Count in order by tens to draw the path the boy takes to the store.

38

Place Value: Tens And Ones

Directions: Write the answers in the correct spaces.

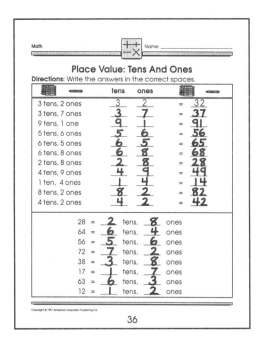

	tens	ones	
3 tens, 2 ones	3	2	= 32
3 tens, 7 ones	3	7	= 37
9 tens, 1 one	9	1	= 91
5 tens, 6 ones	5	6	= 56
6 tens, 5 ones	6	5	= 65
6 tens, 8 ones	6	8	= 68
2 tens, 8 ones	2	8	= 28
4 tens, 9 ones	4	9	= 49
1 ten, 4 ones	1	4	= 14
8 tens, 2 ones	8	2	= 82
4 tens, 2 ones	4	2	= 42

28 = **2** tens, **8** ones
64 = **6** tens, **4** ones
56 = **5** tens, **6** ones
72 = **7** tens, **2** ones
38 = **3** tens, **8** ones
17 = **1** tens, **7** ones
63 = **6** tens, **3** ones
12 = **1** tens, **2** ones

36

Counting By Fives

Directions: Count by fives to draw the path to the playground.

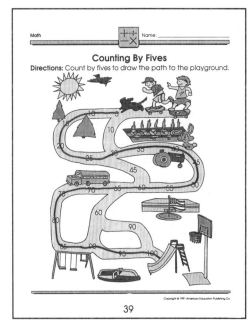

39

Ordinal Numbers

Ordinal numbers are used to indicate order in a series, such as **first**, **second**, or **third**.

Directions: Draw a line to the picture that corresponds to the ordinal number in the left column.

eighth
third
sixth
ninth
seventh
second
fourth
first
fifth
tenth

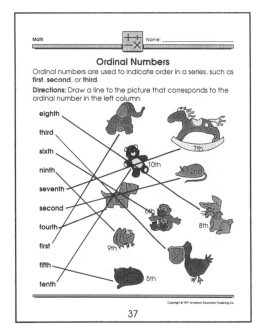

37

Fractions

Directions: Color half of each object.

Example:

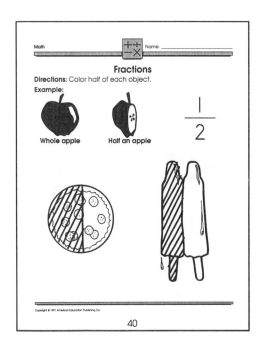

Whole apple   Half an apple $\frac{1}{2}$

40

79

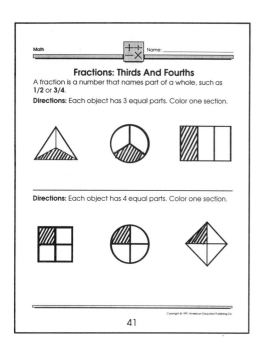

Fractions: Thirds And Fourths

A fraction is a number that names part of a whole, such as 1/2 or 3/4.

Directions: Each object has 3 equal parts. Color one section.

Directions: Each object has 4 equal parts. Color one section.

41

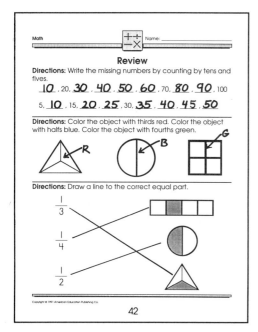

Review

Directions: Write the missing numbers by counting by tens and fives.

10 , 20 , 30 , 40 , 50 , 60 , 70 , 80 , 90 , 100

5 , 10 , 15 , 20 , 25 , 30 , 35 , 40 , 45 , 50

Directions: Color the object with thirds red. Color the object with halves blue. Color the object with fourths green.

Directions: Draw a line to the correct equal part.

$\frac{1}{3}$

$\frac{1}{4}$

$\frac{1}{2}$

42

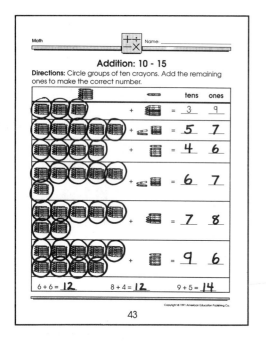

Addition: 10 - 15

Directions: Circle groups of ten crayons. Add the remaining ones to make the correct number.

				tens	ones
	+		=	3	9
	+		=	5	7
	+		=	4	6
	+		=	6	7
	+		=	7	8
	+		=	9	6

6 + 6 = 12   8 + 4 = 12   9 + 5 = 14

43

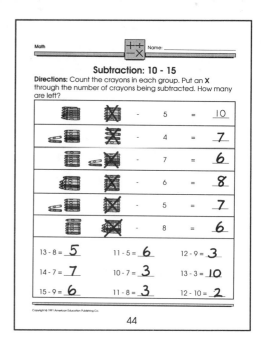

Subtraction: 10 - 15

Directions: Count the crayons in each group. Put an **X** through the number of crayons being subtracted. How many are left?

		-	5	=	10
		-	4	=	7
		-	7	=	6
		-	6	=	8
		-	5	=	7
		-	8	=	6

13 - 8 = 5   11 - 5 = 6   12 - 9 = 3

14 - 7 = 7   10 - 7 = 3   13 - 3 = 10

15 - 9 = 6   11 - 8 = 3   12 - 10 = 2

44

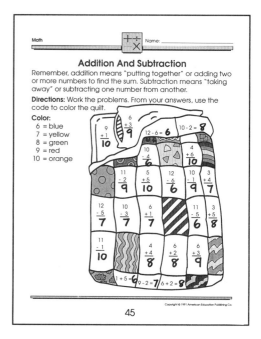

Addition And Subtraction

Remember, addition means "putting together" or adding two or more numbers to find the sum. Subtraction means "taking away" or subtracting one number from another.

Directions: Work the problems. From your answers, use the code to color the quilt.

Color:
6 = blue
7 = yellow
8 = green
9 = red
10 = orange

45

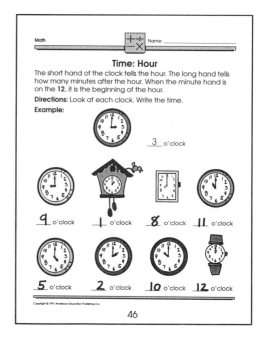

Time: Hour

The short hand of the clock tells the hour. The long hand tells how many minutes after the hour. When the minute hand is on the **12**, it is the beginning of the hour.

Directions: Look at each clock. Write the time.

Example:

3 o'clock

9 o'clock   1 o'clock   8 o'clock   11 o'clock

5 o'clock   2 o'clock   10 o'clock   12 o'clock

46

Time: Hour, Half-Hour

The short hand of the clock tells the hour. The long hand tells how many minutes after the hour. When the minute hand is on the **6**, it is on the half-hour. A half-hour is thirty minutes. It is written **:30**, such as **5:30**.

Directions: Look at each clock. Write the time.

Example:

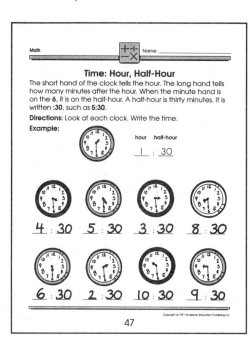

hour   half-hour
_1_ : _30_

_4_ : _30_   _5_ : _30_   _3_ : _30_   _8_ : _30_

_6_ : _30_   _2_ : _30_   _10_ : _30_   _9_ : _30_

47

Time: Hour, Half-Hour

Directions: Draw the hands on each clock to show the correct time.

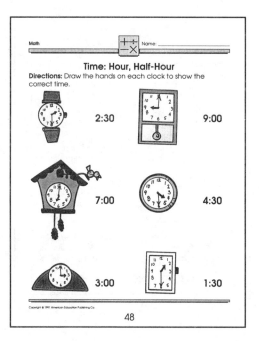

2:30   9:00

7:00   4:30

3:00   1:30

48

Money: Penny And Nickel

A penny is worth one cent. It is written **1¢** or **$.01**. A nickel is worth five cents. It is written **5¢** or **$.05**.

Directions: Count the money and write the answers.

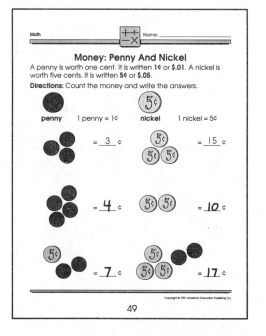

penny   1 penny = 1¢   nickel   1 nickel = 5¢

= _3_ ¢   = _15_ ¢

= _4_ ¢   = _10_ ¢

= _7_ ¢   = _17_ ¢

49

Review

Directions: What time is it?

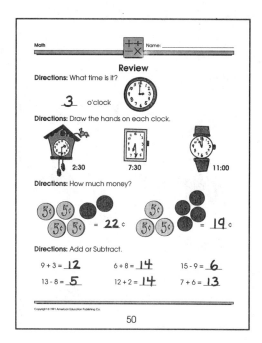

_3_   o'clock

Directions: Draw the hands on each clock.

2:30   7:30   11:00

Directions: How much money?

= _22_ ¢   = _19_ ¢

Directions: Add or Subtract.

9 + 3 = _12_   6 + 8 = _14_   15 - 9 = _6_

13 - 8 = _5_   12 + 2 = _14_   7 + 6 = _13_

50

Picture Problems: Addition 0 - 9

Directions: Work the number problem under each picture.

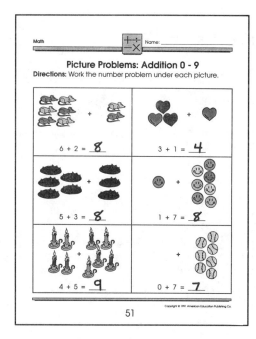

6 + 2 = _8_   3 + 1 = _4_

5 + 3 = _8_   1 + 7 = _8_

4 + 5 = _9_   0 + 7 = _7_

51

Picture Problems: Addition 0 - 9

Directions: Work the number problem under each picture.

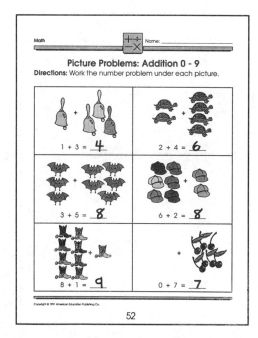

1 + 3 = _4_   2 + 4 = _6_

3 + 5 = _8_   6 + 2 = _8_

8 + 1 = _9_   0 + 7 = _7_

52

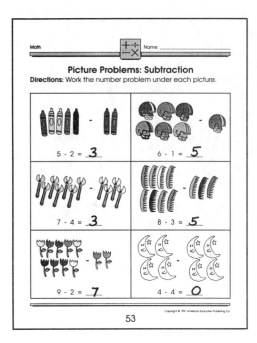

Picture Problems: Subtraction
Directions: Work the number problem under each picture.

5 - 2 = **3**

6 - 1 = **5**

7 - 4 = **3**

8 - 3 = **5**

9 - 2 = **7**

4 - 4 = **0**

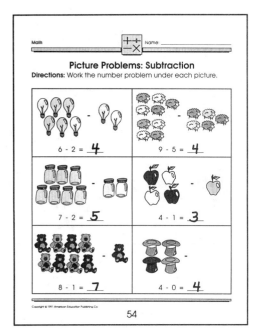

Picture Problems: Subtraction
Directions: Work the number problem under each picture.

6 - 2 = **4**

9 - 5 = **4**

7 - 2 = **5**

4 - 1 = **3**

8 - 1 = **7**

4 - 0 = **4**

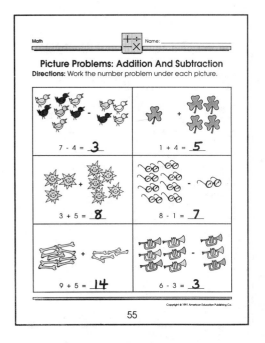

Picture Problems: Addition And Subtraction
Directions: Work the number problem under each picture.

7 - 4 = **3**

1 + 4 = **5**

3 + 5 = **8**

8 - 1 = **7**

9 + 5 = **14**

6 - 3 = **3**

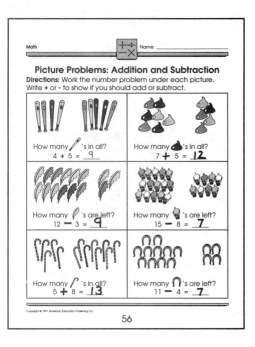

Picture Problems: Addition and Subtraction
Directions: Work the number problem under each picture.
Write + or - to show if you should add or subtract.

How many /'s in all?
4 + 5 = **9**

How many 🍫's in all?
7 **+** 5 = **12**

How many /'s are left?
12 **-** 3 = **9**

How many 🦐's are left?
15 - 8 = **7**

How many /'s in all?
5 **+** 8 = **13**

How many ∩'s are left?
11 **-** 4 = **7**

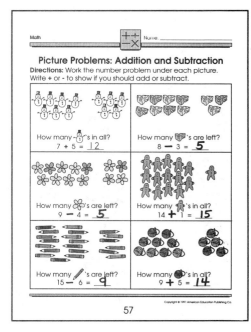

Picture Problems: Addition and Subtraction
Directions: Work the number problem under each picture.
Write + or - to show if you should add or subtract.

How many ⛄'s in all?
7 + 5 = **12**

How many 🦇's are left?
8 **-** 3 = **5**

How many ✿'s are left?
9 **-** 4 = **5**

How many 🎐's in all?
14 **+** 1 = **15**

How many /'s are left?
15 - 6 = **9**

How many 🥚's in all?
9 **+** 5 = **14**

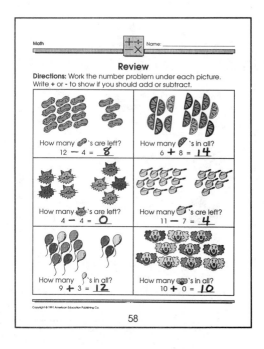

Review
Directions: Work the number problem under each picture.
Write + or - to show if you should add or subtract.

How many 🥜's are left?
12 **-** 4 = **8**

How many 🍊's in all?
6 **+** 8 = **14**

How many 🐱's are left?
4 - 4 = **0**

How many 🌷's are left?
11 **-** 7 = **4**

How many 🎈's in all?
9 **+** 3 = **12**

How many 🤡's in all?
10 **+** 0 = **10**

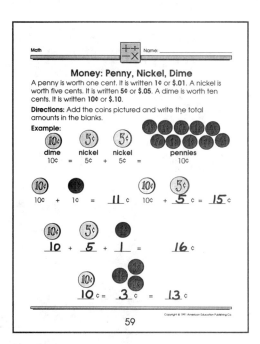

Money: Penny, Nickel, Dime

A penny is worth one cent. It is written 1¢ or $.01. A nickel is worth five cents. It is written 5¢ or $.05. A dime is worth ten cents. It is written 10¢ or $.10.

Directions: Add the coins pictured and write the total amounts in the blanks.

Example:

dime	nickel	nickel	pennies
10¢ =	5¢ +	5¢ =	10¢

10¢ + 1¢ = __11__¢   10¢ + __5__¢ = __15__¢

__10__ + __5__ + __1__ = __16__¢

__10__¢ = __3__¢ = __13__¢

59

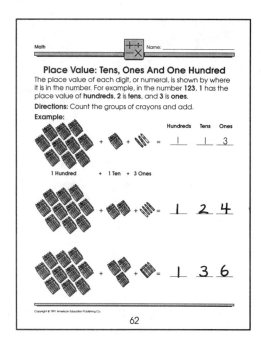

Place Value: Tens, Ones And One Hundred

The place value of each digit, or numeral, is shown by where it is in the number. For example, in the number **123**, **1** has the place value of **hundreds**, **2** is **tens**, and **3** is **ones**.

Directions: Count the groups of crayons and add.

Example:

	Hundreds	Tens	Ones
+ + =	1	1	3

1 Hundred   +   1 Ten   +   3 Ones

+ + = __1__ __2__ __4__

+ + = __1__ __3__ __6__

62

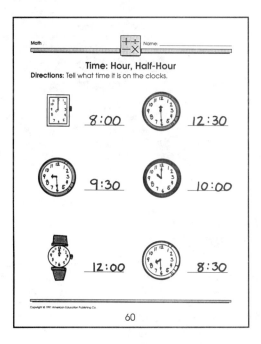

Time: Hour, Half-Hour

Directions: Tell what time it is on the clocks.

__8:00__   __12:30__

__9:30__   __10:00__

__12:00__   __8:30__

60

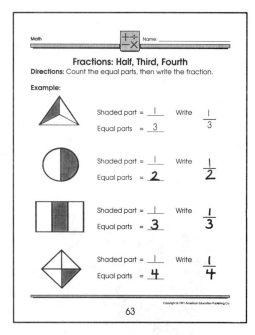

Fractions: Half, Third, Fourth

Directions: Count the equal parts, then write the fraction.

Example:

Shaded part = __1__   Write $\frac{1}{3}$
Equal parts = __3__

Shaded part = __1__   Write $\frac{1}{2}$
Equal parts = __2__

Shaded part = __1__   Write $\frac{1}{3}$
Equal parts = __3__

Shaded part = __1__   Write $\frac{1}{4}$
Equal parts = __4__

63

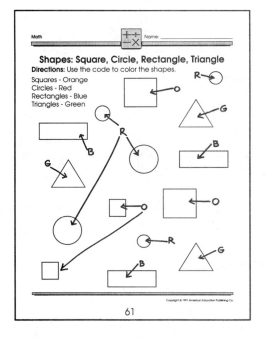

Shapes: Square, Circle, Rectangle, Triangle

Directions: Use the code to color the shapes.

Squares - Orange
Circles - Red
Rectangles - Blue
Triangles - Green

61

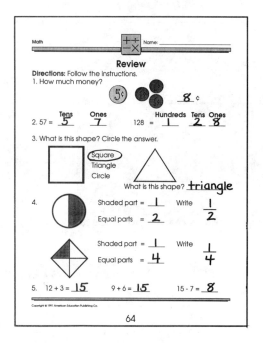

Review

Directions: Follow the instructions.

1. How much money?   __8__¢

2. 57 = | Tens | Ones | 128 = | Hundreds | Tens | Ones |
        | 5 | 7 | | 1 | 2 | 8 |

3. What is this shape? Circle the answer.

(Square)
Triangle
Circle

What is this shape? __triangle__

4. Shaded part = __1__   Write $\frac{1}{2}$
   Equal parts = __2__

   Shaded part = __1__   Write $\frac{1}{4}$
   Equal parts = __4__

5. 12 + 3 = __15__   9 + 6 = __15__   15 - 7 = __8__

64

83

INTRODUCING
BRIGHTER CHILD™ SOFTWARE!

BRIGHTER CHILD ™ SOFTWARE for Windows

These colorful and exciting programs teach basic skills in an entertaining way. They are based on the best selling BRIGHTER CHILD™ workbooks, written and designed by experts who are also parents. Sound is included to facilitate learning, but it is not nesessary to run these programs. BRIGHTER CHILD™ software has received many outstanding reviews and awards. All Color! Easy to use!

The following programs are each sold separately in a 3.5 disk format.

Reading & Phonics Grade 1	*Reading Grade 2*	*Reading Grade 3*
Math Grade 1	*Math Grade 2*	*Math Grade 3*

CD-ROM Titles!

These new titles combine three grade levels of a subject on one CD-ROM! Each CD contains more than 80 different activities packed with colors and sound.

Reading and Phonics Challenge - CD-ROM Grades 1, 2, 3
Math Challenge - CD-ROM Grades 1, 2, 3

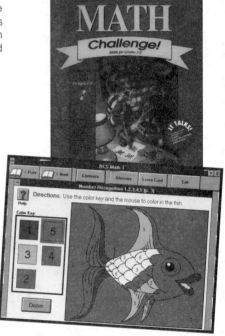

JIM HENSON'S MUPPET™/
BRIGHTER CHILD™ SOFTWARE for Windows™

Based on the best selling Muppet Press™/BRIGHTER CHILD™ Workbooks, these software programs for Windows are designed to teach basic concepts to children in preschool and kindergarten. Children will develop phonics skills and critical and creative thinking skills, and more! No reading is required with a sound card -- the directions are read aloud. The Muppet™ characters are universally known and loved and are recognized as having high educational value.

The following programs are each sold separately in a 3.5 disk format.
Each package contains:

- a program disk with more than 15 full color animated interactive lessons!
- sound is included which facilitates learning.
- Full-color workbook

Beginning Sounds: Phonics	*Letters: Capital & Small*
Same & Different	

CD-ROM Titles

Beginning Reading & Phonics- CD-ROM

This title combines three different MUPPET™/BRIGHTER CHILD™ Software programs -- Beginning Sounds: Phonics, Letters, and Same and Different -- all on one CD-ROM! This valuable software contains more than 50 different activities packed with color, sound, and interactive animation!

Reading & Phonics II- CD-ROM

Three Muppet™ Early Reading Programs on one CD-ROM. Includes *Sorting & Ordering, Thinking Skills,* and *Sound Patterns: More Phonics*

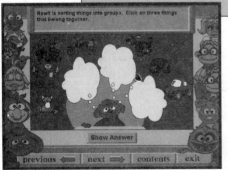

Available at stores everywhere.

OVERVIEW

ENRICHMENT READING is designed to provide children with practice in reading and to increase students' reading abilities. The program consists of six editions, one each for grades 1 through 6. The major areas of reading instruction--word skills, vocabulary, study skills, comprehension, and literary forms--are covered as appropriate at each level.

ENRICHMENT READING provides a wide range of activities that target a variety of skills in each instructional area. The program is unique because it helps children expand their skills in playful ways with games, puzzles, riddles, contests, and stories. The high-interest activities are informative and fun to do.

Home involvement is important to any child's success in school. *ENRICHMENT READING* is the ideal vehicle for fostering home involvement. Every lesson provides specific opportunities for children to work with a parent, a family member, an adult, or a friend.

AUTHORS

Peggy Kaye, the author of *ENRICHMENT READING*, is also an author of *ENRICHMENT MATH* and the author of two parent/teacher resource books, *Games for Reading* and *Games for Math*. Currently, Ms. Kaye divides her time between writing books and tutoring students in reading and math. She has also taught for ten years in New York City public and private schools.

WRITERS

Timothy J. Baehr is a writer and editor of instructional materials on the elementary, secondary, and college levels. Mr. Baehr has also authored an award-winning column on bicycling and a resource book for writers of educational materials.

Cynthia Benjamin is a writer of reading instructional materials, television scripts, and original stories. Ms. Benjamin has also tutored students in reading at the New York University Reading Institute.

Russell Ginns is a writer and editor of materials for a children's science and nature magazine. Mr. Ginn's speciality is interactive materials, including games, puzzles, and quizzes.

WHY ENRICHMENT READING?

Enrichment and parental involvement are both crucial to children's success in school, and educators recognize the important role work done at home plays in the educational process. Enrichment activities give children opportunities to practice, apply, and expand their reading skills, while encouraging them to think while they read. *ENRICHMENT READING* offers exactly this kind of opportunity. Each lesson focuses on an important reading skill and involves children in active learning. Each lesson will entertain and delight children.

When children enjoy their lessons and are involved in the activities, they are naturally alert and receptive to learning. They understand more. They remember more. All children enjoy playing games, having contests, and solving puzzles. They like reading interesting stories, amusing stories, jokes, and riddles. Activities such as these get children involved in reading. This is why these kinds of activities form the core of *ENRICHMENT READING.*

Each lesson consists of two parts. Children complete the first part by themselves. The second part is completed together with a family member, an adult, or a friend. *ENRICHMENT READING* activities do not require people at home to teach reading. Instead, the activities involve everyone in enjoyable reading games and interesting language experiences.

ENRICHMENT ANSWER KEY
Math Grade 1

Grade 1 Math — answers will vary.

ENRICHMENT ANSWER KEY
Math Grade 1

Grade 1 Math — answers will vary.